JUNIOR BIOS

Donald Glover

BY HAYLEY NORRIS

Enslow
PUBLISHING

Please visit our website, www.enslow.com. For a free color catalog of all our high-quality books, call toll free 1-800-398-2504 or fax 1-877-980-4454.

Library of Congress Cataloging-in-Publication Data

Names: Norris, Hayley, author.
Title: Donald Glover / Hayley Norris.
Description: New York : Enslow Publishing, [2021] | Series: Junior bios |
    Includes index. | Identifiers: LCCN 2020005098 | ISBN 9781978518872 (library binding) | ISBN 9781978518858 (paperback) | ISBN 9781978518865 (6 Pack) | ISBN 9781978518889 (ebook)
Subjects: LCSH: Glover, Donald, 1983–Juvenile literature. |
    Actors–United States–Biography–Juvenile literature. |
    Musicians–United States–Biography–Juvenile literature.
Classification: LCC PN2287.G556 N67 2021 | DDC 791.4302/8092–dc23
LC record available at https://lccn.loc.gov/2020005098

First Edition

Published in 2021 by
Enslow Publishing
101 West 23rd Street, Suite #240
New York, NY 10011

Copyright © 2021 Enslow Publishing

Designer: Sarah Liddell
Editor: Kate Mikoley

Photo credits: Cover, p. 1 (Donald Glover) DFree/Shutterstock.com; cover, p. 1 (photo frame) Aleksandr Andrushkiv/Shutterstock.com; marble texture used throughout HardtIllustrations/Shutterstock.com; lined paper texture used throughout Mtsaride/Shutterstock.com; watercolor texture used throughout solarbird/Shutterstock.com; p. 5 Joseph Okpako/Contributor/WireImage/Getty Images; p. 7 Lester Cohen/Contributor/WireImage/Getty Images; p. 9 Angela Weiss/Stringer/Getty Images Entertainment/Getty Images; p. 11 Frederick M. Brown/Stringer/Getty Images Entertainment/Getty Images; p. 12 Ethan Miller/Staff/Getty Images Entertainment/Getty Images; p. 15 Jason LaVeris/Contributor/FilmMagic/Getty Images; p. 17 Mark Metcalfe/Stringer/Getty Images Entertainment/Getty Images; p. 19 Alberto E. Rodriguez/Stringer/Getty Images Entertainment/Getty Images.

All rights reserved. No part of this book may be reproduced in any form without permission in writing from the publisher, except by a reviewer.

Printed in the United States of America

Some of the images in this book illustrate individuals who are models. The depictions do not imply actual situations or events.

CPSIA compliance information: Batch #BS20ENS: For further information contact Enslow Publishing, New York, New York, at 1-800-542-2595.

Find us on

Contents

A Well-Rounded Entertainer 4

Growing Up. 6

On to Acting 8

Big Breaks 10

All About *Atlanta* 14

Making More Music 16

Coming Full Circle 18

What's Next? 20

Donald's Timeline 21

Glossary 22

For More Information 23

Index 24

Words in the glossary appear in **bold** type the first time they are used in the text.

A Well-Rounded Entertainer

When someone knows about a lot of different subjects or takes part in many activities, you might hear others call them well-rounded. When it comes to people working in the entertainment business today, Donald Glover is certainly one of the most well-rounded.

Donald is an actor, writer, musician, and **comedian**. He's worked on many popular TV shows and movies. As a musician, he goes by the name Childish Gambino. His songs have earned him multiple Grammy Awards and even more **nominations**. When it comes to working in show business, it seems there's not much Donald Glover hasn't mastered.

DONALD USED AN ONLINE NICKNAME MAKER TO COME UP WITH HIS STAGE NAME, CHILDISH GAMBINO.

Growing Up

On September 25, 1983, Donald Glover was born on a U.S. Air Force base in California. When he was young, his family moved to Stone Mountain, Georgia, about 20 miles (32 km) outside of Atlanta. He was raised there with his siblings. Donald has one **biological** brother and one biological sister. He also has two adopted siblings and grew up with **foster children** who his parents took in.

FACTS BEHIND THE FIGURE

Without much TV, Donald used his imagination a lot. He would put on his own puppet shows and plays at home for his family.

DONALD'S YOUNGER BROTHER, STEPHEN, IS A WRITER AND **PRODUCER**. THEY'VE WORKED TOGETHER ON DONALD'S TV SHOW ATLANTA.

His mother, Beverly, managed a day care. His father, also named Donald, worked in a post office. He was raised in a religion, called Jehovah's Witnesses, that didn't allow much TV or movie watching.

On to Acting

Even though most TV and movies were off limits, Donald's father would take him to see *Star Wars* movies. These became a favorite for him. Donald would also secretly record the sound from the TV show *The Simpsons*. He'd later listen to and retell the show with his brother.

In college, Donald joined an improvisational, or improv, comedy group. Improvisation is performing without preparing ahead of time. In improv comedy, actors perform funny pieces that they make up as they go.

IN HIGH SCHOOL, DONALD'S CLASSMATES VOTED HIM "MOST LIKELY TO WRITE FOR THE SIMPSONS."

Donald went to a high school for performing arts. At school, he performed in musicals and plays and took dance classes. After finishing high school, Donald went to college at New York University's Tisch School of the Arts. He studied dramatic writing and graduated in 2006.

Big Breaks

After college, Donald got a job writing for a TV show called *30 Rock*. He was only 23. The show's creator, Tina Fey, had seen some of the work he'd done with his improv group. Donald worked as a writer on the show for about three years and even appeared on screen in a few episodes.

In His Own Words
"You have to be real with yourself … People are too concerned with making everything look nice and calm and pretty."

ON *COMMUNITY*, DONALD WAS KNOWN FOR BEING A GOOD IMPROVISER. SOMETIMES, THE **SCRIPT** WOULD JUST DIRECT HIM TO SAY SOMETHING FUNNY, BECAUSE THE WRITERS KNEW HE WOULD COME UP WITH SOMETHING!

In 2009, Donald left the show to move to Los Angeles, California. Just six days after quitting *30 Rock*, Donald had a new job! He was cast as one of the main characters in a TV show called *Community*.

11

WHILE DONALD WAS ON *COMMUNITY* AND COMING OUT WITH NEW MUSIC, HE WAS ALSO KEEPING HIMSELF BUSY WITH A FEW OTHER ACTING JOBS, SUCH AS APPEARANCES ON THE TV SHOW *GIRLS*, WRITING, AND MAKING MUSIC VIDEOS.

During his time on *Community*, Donald was also working on his music and his writing. He was doing stand-up, a type of comedy where the performer does a show on stage in front of an **audience**, too.

Donald had been making music for a while, but his first big album came in 2011, under his stage name Childish Gambino. The rap album, called *Camp*, came out the same week a stand-up special of his was shown on Comedy Central. Donald was becoming well-known for his many talents. In 2013, he came out with another album called *Because the Internet*.

Because the Internet earned Donald his first two Grammy nominations. The album was nominated in 2015 for Best Rap Album. His song "3005" was also nominated for Best Rap Performance.

All About Atlanta

Donald's last episode of *Community* aired in 2014, but by 2013, he was already ready for more than writing for or acting in a TV show. He wanted to create one of his own. That's when he came up with the idea for *Atlanta*, a show about the rap scene in Atlanta, Georgia.

FACTS BEHIND THE FIGURE

Atlanta is a comedy, but it can also be serious. The characters on the show deal with issues related to important topics, such as **poverty** and race.

DONALD HAS EARNED A NUMBER OF AWARDS FOR HIS WORK ON ATLANTA. IN 2017, HE WON EMMYS FOR ACTING AND DIRECTING. HE WAS THE FIRST AFRICAN AMERICAN TO WIN AN EMMY FOR DIRECTING A COMEDY SERIES.

Donald signed a deal with the TV network FX saying he would write, star in, and produce the show. The first episode came out in 2016. It quickly gained fans. Donald played the lead character, Earn, who manages his cousin's rap career.

Making More Music

In 2016, Childish Gambino came out with another album, called *Awaken, My Love!* In 2018, he came out with a song called "This Is America." The song quickly became a hit and got a lot of attention. While Donald hasn't spoken too much about the meaning behind the song or its video, many people saw it as a statement about **violence**, race, and being a black person in the United States.

In His Own Words
"I hope in general that my music allows somebody to follow what they really like doing ... I just like learning stuff. I like doing stuff. And I feel like everybody can definitely do it."

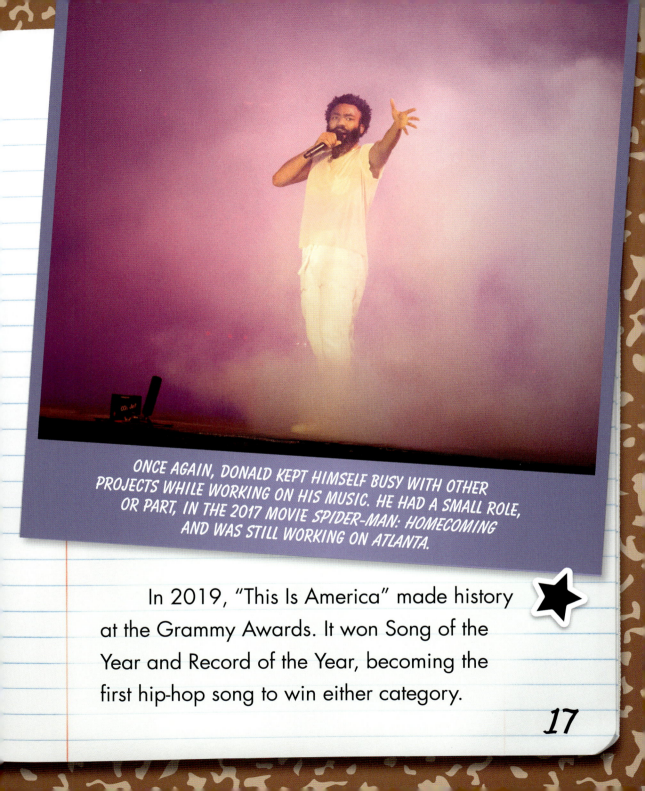

ONCE AGAIN, DONALD KEPT HIMSELF BUSY WITH OTHER PROJECTS WHILE WORKING ON HIS MUSIC. HE HAD A SMALL ROLE, OR PART, IN THE 2017 MOVIE *SPIDER-MAN: HOMECOMING* AND WAS STILL WORKING ON *ATLANTA*.

In 2019, "This Is America" made history at the Grammy Awards. It won Song of the Year and Record of the Year, becoming the first hip-hop song to win either category.

Coming Full Circle

In 2018, Donald had a role in the movie *Solo: A Star Wars Story*. He played Lando Calrissian, a character he had watched in earlier *Star Wars* movies—some of the only movies he was allowed to watch when he was a kid. Donald has said he always loved the character when he was young and even remembers having a toy figure of Lando!

FACTS BEHIND THE FIGURE

When Donald heard there was going to be a Han Solo movie, he told his **agent** he wanted to play Lando. At first, his agent told him he didn't think he would get the job. That made Donald want it even more!

18

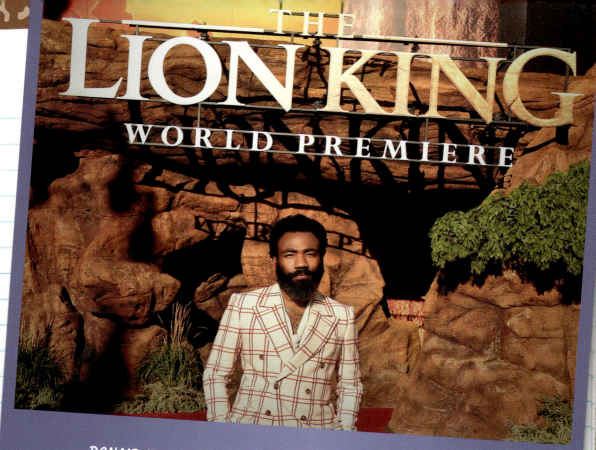

DONALD HAS SAID THAT AS A KID, MUSIC FROM THE ORIGINAL LION KING MOVIE INSPIRED HIM TO WRITE HIS OWN SONGS!

In 2019, Donald was in another remake of a movie from his childhood: *The Lion King*. He did the voice for Simba in the computer-**animated** retelling of the hit movie from 1994.

What's Next?

From making music, acting, and writing to producing, directing, and creating his own show, there's not much in show business Donald hasn't done and succeeded at. His work has touched on important issues, **influenced** the public, and won many awards. Plus, he has one of the most well-rounded careers of anyone in the entertainment business.

What's next for the man who has seemingly tried it all? Only time will tell! But if Donald Glover's past work is any hint at the things he'll do next, it's pretty safe to guess that whatever he does will be great!

Donald's Timeline

1983: Donald is born on September 25.

2006: Donald graduates from New York University's Tisch School of the Arts.
He starts writing for *30 Rock*.

2009: Donald leaves *30 Rock* and starts working on *Community*.

2011: Childish Gambino's album *Camp* comes out.

2013: Childish Gambino's album *Because the Internet* comes out.

2016: The first episode of *Atlanta* comes out.
Childish Gambino's album *Awaken, My Love!* comes out.

2018: Childish Gambino's hit song "This Is America" is released.
Donald plays Lando Calrissian in *Solo: A Star Wars Story*.

2019: "This Is America" becomes the first hip-hop song to win a Grammy for Song of the Year and Record of the Year.
Donald voices Simba in *The Lion King*.

Glossary

agent A person who helps performers get jobs.
animated Consisting of drawings or computer images that appear to move.
audience The people who watch a performance.
biological Related through birth.
comedian A person who performs comedy, or works meant to make people laugh.
foster children Children who live with and are cared for by adults who are not their parents for a period of time because their parents cannot care for them.
influence To have an effect on.
nomination The act of being suggested for an honor.
poverty The state of being poor.
producer Someone who organizes, supervises, and helps pay for the making of a movie or TV show.
script A written plan for a show or movie.
violence The use of force to harm someone.

For More Information

Books

Wilkins, Jonathan. *Solo: A Star Wars Story: The Ultimate Guide.* London, England: Titan Magazines, 2018.

Wood, Alix. *Be an Actor.* New York, NY: PowerKids Press, 2018.

Websites

Donald Glover Biography
www.biography.com/actor/donald-glover
Learn more about Donald's life by reading this short biography.

Star Wars: Solo
www.starwars.com/films/solo
Find out more about the *Star Wars* film Donald was in and watch clips from the movie.

Publisher's note to educators and parents: Our editors have carefully reviewed these websites to ensure that they are suitable for students. Many websites change frequently, however, and we cannot guarantee that a site's future contents will continue to meet our high standards of quality and educational value. Be advised that students should be closely supervised whenever they access the internet.

Index

actor, 4, 8, 12, 14, 15, 20
albums, 13, 16, 21
Atlanta, 7, 14, 15, 17, 21
brother, 6, 7, 8
Calrissian, Lando, 18, 21
college, 8, 9, 10
Community, 11, 12, 14, 21
directing, 15, 20
Emmys, 15
family, 6
father, 7, 8
Gambino, Childish, 4, 5, 13, 16, 21
Grammy Awards, 4, 17
high school, 9
imagination, 6
Lion King, The, 19, 21
mother, 7
movies, 4, 7, 8, 17, 18, 19
music, 12, 13, 16, 17, 19, 20
race, 14, 16
religion, 7
Simba, 19, 21
Simpsons, The, 8, 9
stand-up, 12, 13
Star Wars, 8, 18, 21
30 Rock, 10, 11, 21
"This Is America", 16, 17, 21
writing, 9, 10, 12, 14, 20, 21